RE 623H MOLLIES

Distributed in the UNITED STATES by T.F.H. Publications, Inc., 1 TFH Plaza, Neptune City, NJ 07753; on the Internet at www.tfh.com; in CANADA by Rolf C. Hagen Inc., 3225 Sartelon St., Montreal, Quebec H4R 1E8; Pet Trade by H & L Pet Supplies Inc., 27 Kingston Crescent, Kitchener, Ontario N2B 2T6; in ENGLAND by T.F.H. Publications, PO Box 74, Havant PO9 5TT; in AUSTRALIA AND THE SOUTH PACIFIC by T.F.H. (Australia), Pty. Ltd., Box 149, Brookvale 2100 N.S.W., Australia; in NEW ZEALAND by Brooklands Aquarium Ltd., 5 McGiven Drive, New Plymouth, RD1 New Zealand; in SOUTH AFRICA by Rolf C. Hagen S.A. (PTY.) LTD., P.O. Box 201199, Durban North 4016, South Africa; in JAPAN by T.F.H. Publications. Published by T.F.H. Publications, Inc.

MANUFACTURED IN THE
UNITED STATES OF AMERICA
BY T.F.H. PUBLICATIONS, INC.

INTRODUCTION

At a pet supply trade show, one particular manufacturer of artificial aquarium plants put together a breathtaking display. Carefully laid out in a 55-gallon aquarium were the newest of aquarium plants, glowing with color, set in stark white gravel. The fish that were selected to accompany the company's featured product were shimmering white, with pearlescent scales, waving dorsal fins and trident-like tail fins. These fish swam majestically through the set-up as if they were manufactured especially for this company's particular display.

More than likely they were chosen by the display's designer, who must have known how the chosen fish's comportment and stylishness would enhance the display rather than overwhelming it. What is this fish that I've already begun to rave about? Obviously, it's a molly of one sort or another. The particular mollies chosen for complementing the manufacturer's display of artificial aquarium plants were silver sailfin mollies.

Poecilia velifera, the Silver Sailfin Molly. Bred by Guy Buzbee's Tropical Fish Farm. Photo by Dr. Harry Grier courtesy of FTFFA.

The silver sailfin is but one color variation of the fish. There are black varieties and black and white marbled, brown, brown and white marbled and some other variations on those themes, as well as an orange. The "sailfin" is not the only finnage variety of molly available either. There are short-finned mollies, and there are hi-finned and lyretailed mollies also. There also is a molly with a bulbous abdominal region and foreshortened body; referred to as the balloon molly, it is available in a number of different colors.

Given the proper care, mollies can be hardy fishes. But mollies often are, unfortunately, chosen by first-time aquarium hobbyists ignorant of their special needs, and in the hands of the inexperienced mollies are the reverse of hardy; instead, they're miserably sickly. I'll bet you a can of fish food that many of the first-time aquarists who start out with mollies in their aquarium can tell you horror stories about mollies' sickliness. These novices probably had their first experience with the disease known as "ich" as it attacked and quickly wiped out their new mollies.

Poecilia velifera, the Chocolate Lyretail Molly (male). Fish produced by Buzbee's Tropical Fish Farm. Photo by Edward Taylor.

The relatively inexpensive prices of most mollies, combined with their nice looks and live-bearing characteristics, make these fishes hard to resist. The unfortunate part is that very few first-timers are aware that most of the popular mollies originally came from brackish or even pure salt water. I realize that water conditions in the waters that a species originally came from might have no bearing on the conditions needed by mollies derived from stock that has been housed and bred under non-natural captive conditions for many years, but it's still my experience that with no salt whatsoever in the aquarium mollies will not thrive and may even perish after a bout with one disease or another. In the chapter on water quality I will go into more detail on this subject.

The mollies are fruitful multipliers, and their status as bearers of living young (as opposed to being egg-layers) makes them appealing to children and adults alike. This adds to their desirability on the market. And it should, because being able to get your fish to reproduce themselves successfully while they're in your care adds a new dimension of enjoyment to the hobby. To promote this process does not take an incredible amount of skill or knowledge. It does, however, take a little bit of learning on the keeper's part. This book will attempt to give you that little bit of learning.

***Poecilia latipinna*, the Salt-and-Pepper Sailfin Molly, also called the Panda Molly by its breeder. Photo by Dr. Harry Grier courtesy of FTFFA.**

Once you've gawked at the magnificence of mollies through the photographs presented here and soaked up the information provided, I am sure you will be an

Poecilia velifera, the Milk Chocolate Lyretail Molly (male) produced by Buzbee's Tropical Fish Farm. Photo by Edward Taylor.

instant molly fan. Your next step will be examining or re-examining specimens offered for sale at your local aquarium store. At that point you'll be taking steps to make a spot in your home for these remarkable creatures. If nothing else, you'll be sure to come away with a new-found respect for mollies.

Poecilia velifera, the Sunset Balloon Molly (male). Fish produced by 5-D Tropicals. Photo by Edward Taylor.

A pair of Green Balloon Mollies. The female is the uppermost fish and the black in her abdomen indicates imminent birth. The black is actually the eyes of the unborn young. This variety is a bit more sensitive to proper water quality.

Poecilia sphenops, the Sunburst Molly (male). Fish produced by Moonlight Fishery. Photo by Edward Taylor.

adverse conditions of a newly set up saltwater aquarium. It can be rough on the guinea pig mollies, of course, but not always.

HARDNESS

Water hardness is the measure of dissolved minerals, mostly calcium and magnesium, present in the water. Hardness can vary depending on the source of the water and the makeup of the substrate it flows over. Inasmuch as hardness and marine and/or brackish water go hand in hand, water hardness can be a non-factor in your molly's aquarium so long as you are providing the correct amount of sodium salts in the aquarium.

It would be smart to make use of commercially available marine salt mixes used for saltwater tanks, as they are supplemented with other elements that your mollies will benefit from. These salts will increase your water's hardness as well as its saltiness.

SALINITY

Salinity is often thought of as being interchangeable with specific gravity, because the density of the water is determined at least partly by the amount of dissolved salts in the water; the temperature of the water is another factor that plays a part in determining the specific gravity. All other things being equal, the greater the salt content, the higher the specific gravity. In general, seawater has a specific gravity of about 1.022 to 1.025 as measured with a hydrometer, depending on where and when the measurement is made. The recommended level for mollies would be significantly lower. The easiest formulation would be to just add one teaspoon of non-iodized salt per gallon of water for the desired level needed to keep mollies healthy. Some hobbyists would consider this to be too much salt to add, but it's the quantity I use in all-molly tanks with good results. But keep in mind that although the addition of salt can be a good thing for those mollies whose natural habitats are brackish, it's not going to be appreciated by all other species in the tank if you happen to be housing your mollies in a community aquarium, and it's not going to be appreciated by the tank's plants. Some molly fanciers approach the salt situation from the standpoint of not adding any salt at all unless the fish show signs of discomfort and, if they do, adding just a quarter of a teaspoonful at intervals of a day or so while the fish are still uncomfortable until a maximum of a teaspoonful per gallon is reached.

Poecilia velifera, Golden Sailfin Albino Molly (female). Fish produced by Moonlight Fishery. Photo by Edward Taylor.

SETTING UP

Whether you're keeping mollies in a single-species tank or in a mixed community of other tropicals, you want to adhere to the old aquarium rule of an inch of fish per gallon of water. If you have a fish that's two inches, give him two gallons of water, and so on. A crowded aquarium adds to the stress level of the fish and will lead to the demise of your fish. Mollies in general, but *P. velifera* and *P. latipinna* in particular, are very susceptible to the bad effects resulting from overcrowding.

It is always a good idea to go with as large a tank as you have room for and can afford. Many hobbyists start out with a 10-gallon tank and then quickly outgrow it. You would be better served to start with at least a 20-gallon tank of the long variety. That's a tank that is 12 inches high and 30 inches long. This affords the fish ample swimming room with a comfortable stocking level for the fishkeeper to add to his collection.

You should provide your mollies with clean water and be able to keep it that way. The best way to accomplish this feat is to equip your tank with both an undergravel filter and a mechanical filter. The undergravel filter, powered by a powerhead or an airpump, will oxygenate your gravelbed. This process will facilitate the growth of beneficial

The ideal set up for a molly tank, though the aeration might be too strong. Photo by Ernie Bagur of an aquarium set up by E. Carter.

***Poecilia sphenops*, the Sphenops Salt-and-Pepper Lyretail Molly produced by Buzbee's Tropical Fish Farm. Photo by Edward Taylor.**

bacteria that help to break down fish waste.

A mechanical filter will move the aquarium's water through various filtering media that will draw out visible particulate matter. This will aid in keeping your water crystal clear. To a lesser extent it will serve as an aid to the undergravel filter, as helpful bacteria will form on the filter media as well. Working in combination, these two types of filtration do a good job of keeping the tank clean and the nitrate content down. New developments in the field of aquarium filtration are being made all the time, so check with your dealer to see what can be recommended for the type of tank you set up. You don't want your filtration equipment to be underpowered and unable to handle your tank, but you don't want to spend more than you have to, either.

Mollies are heavily vegetarian in their dietary preferences, so having a tank nicely decorated with living plants will do more than just improve the looks of your fish room; it also will provide good forage for your mollies. That's not to say that the mollies are going to actively chew the plants down like so many aquatic sheep, but they will continually graze on them, picking off algae and perhaps tiny organisms that live in the algae. A well lighted

Poecilia sphenops, the Black-n-Gold Molly. The male is the lower fish; female above. Fish produced by Exotic Fisheries. Photo by Edward Taylor.

aquarium, one that's at least well enough lighted to provide good growth for the plants, will almost always produce some green algal growth at the same time. That's fine in a molly tank, because the mollies will eat the algal growth and benefit from it.

Many fishkeepers, unfortunately, opt to disregard the importance of a tank cover where mollies are concerned. That's too bad, because mollies are entirely capable of jumping. They're not as bad as some other species, but they're far from being as staidly non-jumpy as *Corydoras*, for instance. So when you're selecting your equipment, don't automatically pass up the notion of getting a full-hood reflector instead of a plain strip reflector. And if you use a strip reflector, consider using a cover glass in conjunction with it.

Poecilia latipinna, the Red-splash Sailfin Molly. The color red is very elusive in the *latipinna* species. This nice male was photographed by MP&C Piednoir Aqua Press.

MOLLY TANK MAINTENANCE

When fish produce waste and when organic substances (such as plant debris and uneaten foods) within the tank start to decompose, ammonia is produced. Ammonia build-up can be lethal to your fish. Ammonia build-up combined with the high alkaline levels mollies prefer is certainly deadly. Of course your fish are going to produce wastes, so how does one keep the ammonia from building up?

Remember back to when I was talking about filtration and beneficial bacteria? Those beneficial bacteria are the cornerstones among your building blocks for breaking down fish waste and rendering it less harmful. The gravel bed atop the undergravel filter serves as a host for these bacteria to grow. The undergravel filter system oxygenates the gravel, providing a place to live for oxygen-loving bacteria of the genus *Nitrosomonas*, which break the ammonia down into nitrites, less poisonous than ammonia but still dangerous to fishes. Then other bacteria (*Nitrobacter*) further break down the nitrite into an even less toxic substance, nitrate. At the end of this cycle—called the nitrogen cycle—you can further dilute the nitrate by performing a partial water change.

WATER CHANGES

A water change is when you add water to the aquarium when some has evaporated, right? WRONG!!! A partial water change is the process whereby you remove a part of the water from the aquarium and replace it entirely with new water. This function is performed on a periodic basis. How much you change and how often you change it are always debatable issues with a number of variables. For the purpose of simplicity, my recommendations are general. Keep in mind, though, that they're based on personal experience—and I rarely lose fish to sickness.

I change one-third of my water every two weeks. That is not to say that if you miss a day or two, or even a week for that matter, that your fish are going to go belly up. That shouldn't happen. But if you schedule your water change every month, and then are delayed a week or so, your margin for diluting the ammonia is greatly diminished.

When changing the water, the use of a simple manually operated gravel siphon/vacuum is invaluable. This simple apparatus is great for changing water in tanks up to 30 gallons, more or less. Combine its use with a 5-gallon bucket or water bottle and the change can be performed in minutes. At the same time you can clean up any dirt or debris that has accumulated in and above the gravel bed. If you have a large tank or multiple tanks you may find a water-changing device that hooks directly up to your water source even more useful, but of course there is nothing preventing you from using the regular siphon/vacuum tube from making water changes even in very large tanks; it just takes longer and entails more effort.

Once you remove the water, you'll need to replace it. If you have a small tank and have the ability to store water that can age, this is your best bet. Aged water, or water that has been allowed to sit out of the tap for at least 48 hours, is advantageous in that there is time for any chlorine present to have a chance to dissipate. The presence of chlorine and chloramines in many municipal water systems can kill your fish. You can get rid of chlorine easily enough by storing it as mentioned above, especially if you heavily aerate the water, and you can get rid of it also by using one of the de-chlorinating products available at pet shops and tropical fish specialty stores. Getting rid of chloramine (a mixture of chlorine and ammonia) is trickier, because you can't eliminate the chloramine by simple agitation of the water; you have to use one of the products specifically designed to remove or neutralize chloramine.

***Poecilia sphenops*, the Black Spenops Molly (female). Fish produced by Buzbee's Tropical Fish Farm. Photo by Edward Taylor.**

Poecilia sphenops, a female Harlequin Molly. Produced by Moonlight Fishery. Photograph by Edward Taylor.

Incidentally, you're always better off waiting a little while—a day or two at least—before introducing mollies into a newly set up tank even if you've used a dechlorinating product.

One final word on water changes and mollies. Remember that salt you might have added? Salt does not evaporate. If you top off the water for evaporation, don't add any more salt. It's all still there. Evaporation will have a tendency to make the water saltier and saltier, so you should take this into acount when you make water changes.

TEMPERATURE

Mollies can withstand variations in temperature with no real ill effects, though extremes and sudden relatively large changes have to be avoided. Preferably, you want to maintain a temperature in the range of 77° to 84°F. This is a somewhat slightly higher range than for many other aquarium fishes. If you are mixing mollies with other fishes your best bet would be to stay at the lower end of the mollies' temperature range. You can see why mixing different species from different natural environments can get tricky, which is one reason why it's a good idea to keep mollies in mollies-only tanks.

Another item to take into consideration is the fact that the higher the temperature, the higher the fish's metabolism. This means that the fish will eat a little more, breathe a little faster, and excrete more often. This tells you that keeping fish at a higher temperature range requires a little more attention to those periodic water changes. Try to stick to the "every two weeks" on a consistent basis. The other consideration in keeping fish in water that is warmer than usual is that warm water contains less oxygen than cooler water, so stocking levels should be lower.

Necessarily involved with the subject of temperature ranges is the consideration of aquarium heaters. If you buy your heater strictly on the basis of price, there is an increased likelihood that you could end up cooking your fish. The cheapest heaters have a limited lifespan for providing good service; then they begin to malfunction. Often the malfunction takes the form of having the heater stick while it's in the heating mode, with the result that the water keeps getting warmer and warmer. A stuck heater could send the water temperature into the 90°s F. or higher, essentially cooking your fish. It is for this reason I implore you to invest a little more money and purchase one of the better heating units; they offer advantages in ease of operation as well as in peace of mind. Get a good thermometer, too—and make sure you check it regularly.

***Poecilia sphenops*, a male Black-n-Gold Molly produced by Exotic Fisheries. Photo by Edward Taylor.**

FEEDING MOLLIES

One thing I can't stand is finicky eaters. I like fish that like whatever you feed them. One very nice thing about mollies is their ravenous appetite. It's not that they'll eat you out of house and home, it's just that they seem to enjoy whatever you choose to feed them. This can be a problem, though.

The problem comes into play when the molly keeper becomes complacent and feeds these beautiful fish the same thing, day in and day out. Sure they'll eat a single brand of flake food all day long. You would eat the same thing, too, if that's all you could get. Don't fall into this trap with your mollies, or any other fish for that matter.

Living tubifex worms are among the most easily available of live foods. These worms also come freeze-dried. Photo by Michael Gilroy.

Yes, a good quality flake food makes a good staple for your fish's diet. Supplement your mollies' sustenance with offerings of other food variations. Whenever you can draw upon a supply of live foods make it a point to offer them to your fish. You may not be interested in chopping up earthworms (you might), but they do make a very nutritious meal when offered on occasion. If worm slashing isn't your thing, you can find living fish foods in some aquarium stores. You may come across such types as bloodworms, glassworms and mosquito larvae, to name several. Additionally many stores have live brine shrimp for sale. These are an exceptional treat for your mollies to feast on. When we approach the chapter on breeding, you will see that live food feedings can play an integral part in getting your fish ready to do their thing.

There still might be the squeamish among you who absolutely draw the line when it comes to keeping wormy things in your house. Modern technology has solved that problem as well. All of these items and more are available in frozen or freeze-dried packages. When using the frozen variety, the simplest way to make feeding easy is to allow the package to thaw for 15 minutes or

Adult brine shrimp, *Artemia salina*, may be the best food for mollies. Photo courtesy of San Francisco Bay Brand.

so, just long enough to make the job of cutting it up easier; don't let it thaw out for too long or you won't be able to re-freeze it safely. Cut the slab into little squares, placing them in a baggie to keep in the freezer. When it's feeding time, just take out a square and drop it in.

And if salad's your thing, share some romaine lettuce with your fish friends. If you're an iceberg lettuce eater, forget it. Iceberg lettuce has little nutritional value...for you or your fish. Spinach isn't just for Popeye either...in the tank. You'll notice a difference in your mollies' overall

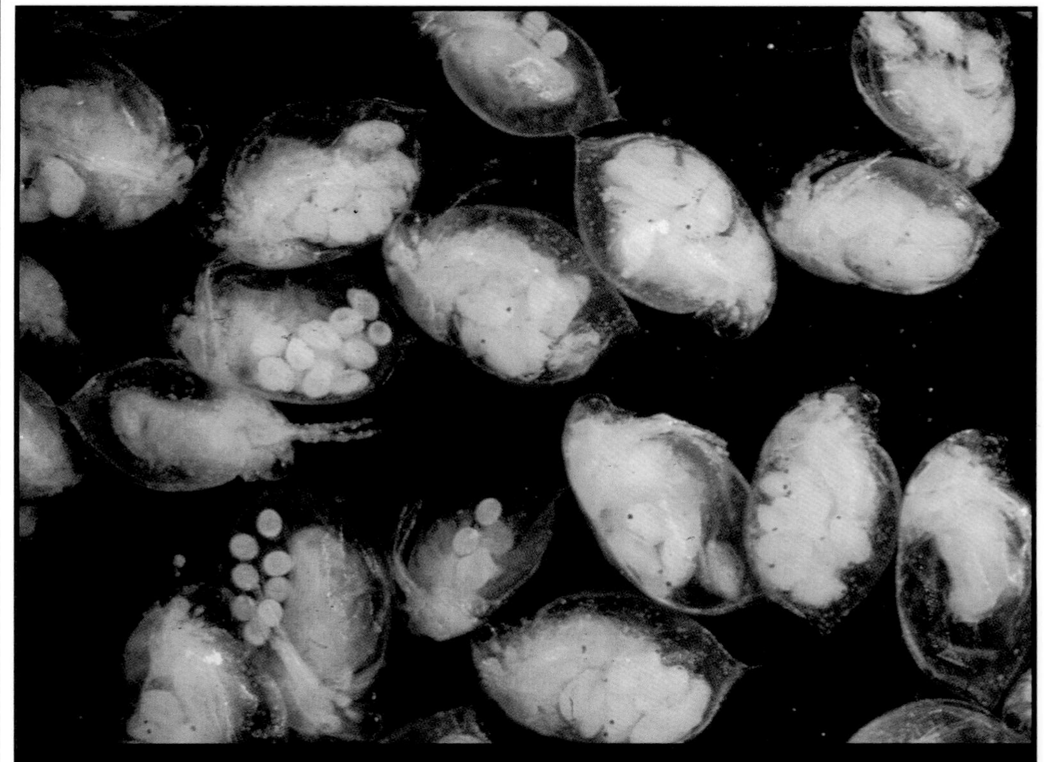

***Daphnia* are one of the best foods for all tropical fishes. Note the eggs inside some of the females. Photo by MP&C Piednoir Aqua Press.**

health and behavior if you consistently feed them the greens they need. Some of the packaged dry foods offered on the aquarium market are designed specifically for mollies and other vegetation-needing fishes, and you should take advantage of them.

In conjunction with flake, live, frozen and freeze-dried varieties, the addition of greens to your mollies' diet is essential for optimum fertility and vitality. This needn't be a chore either. Making peas for dinner? Half-boil some for your mollies. Once they're half-boiled you can store some in the freezer for another feeding.

You should provide a variety of different foods. Nothing could be

Culex pipiens larvae are sold in some pet shops. They are good molly food. Photo by R. Schreiber.

truer when it comes to your fish's nutritional requirements. Variety in the diet will provide your mollies with a gamut of nourishment to make and keep them bright and healthy. Mollies in this condition will also reward you with many subsequent broods of baby mollies. When I say variety I don't mean just different brands of the same basic type of food; I mean different types of prepared foods altogether. Don't use just either flake foods or tableted foods or granulated foods or frozen foods. Keep some of each type on hand and vary the menu.

Bloodworms are really the larvae of *Chironomus*. They are excellent food for mollies if you can get them from your local pet shop. Photo by J. Kadler.

DISEASES

When I first introduced you to mollies I also mentioned this fish is not a beginner's fish, but it is a fish often purchased by beginners. Ultimately, this scenario leads the inexperienced molly keeper to his first bout with *Ichthyophthirius multifiliis*, a parasitic protozoan that causes the malady commmonly referred to as "ich." This is probably the most often encountered malady that will plague your mollies. There are others.

ICH

This parasitic outbreak is also referred to as white spot disease. If you've seen a fish with a case of ich you'll know right away why they call it that. If you've seen a full-blown case of ich you would agree that the fish appears to have been doused with salt. Actually what you have here is a parasite who found a host...your fish. Fear not. If you catch it in time, this irritating and potentially very dangerous pest can be eradicated. But before you embark upon turning your tank into medicine soup, take a minute to figure out why your fish became a victim in the first place.

Fish, as a whole, are very resilient creatures with a nicely defined immune system. What causes this system to break down? Same thing as with you and me...stress. What causes the stress? Often with fish as well as with humans: environmental factors. What is wrong with your fish's environment? Check it out. Check your pH levels, as well as ammonia and hardness. If any of these are out of whack take immediate steps to correct them. The same would hold true with temperature. Water that is too cold will break down the fish's immune system, leaving it open to all sorts of diseases. Check your heater.

Are there fish within your community that are bullies? If the mollies are constantly being harassed by other fish, they are indeed being stressed. Whatever problem you encounter should be rectified as soon as possible. A 33% water change is probably called for.

With ich, there are two ways to cure it: medicinally or naturally. I prefer that latter. Here's what to do. Suspend feeding your fish, and gradually (no more than 5° F. at a time), raise the aquarium temperature to the high 80's. Any additional oxygenation you can provide at this time would be beneficial, since it will help alleviate the results of the water's lessened oxygen content. Adding an airstone or two, depending on the size of the tank, would suffice. The heat will speed up the life cycle of the parasite.

Within 24 hours the parasites should begin falling off the fish.

A perfectly healthy Black Sailfin Molly male, *Poecilia latipinna.* Note the black tips of the mouth. Compare this fish with the fish on the facing page which has a fungus infection.

Don't lower the temperature back quite yet, though, because at this point there still will be microscopic ich cysts still remaining in the tank, getting ready to rupture and spill out thousands of new parasites that will seek to attach themselves to your fish. You want to give them another 48 hours to go through their full life cycle. After a full 72 hours you should lower the temperature, gradually, back to the normal range. At this point your fish and your aquarium should be eradicated of this misery-causing pest. Do another 33% water change, adding a healthy dose of a water de-chlorinator. Some de-chlorinators contain substances that not only will help the fish's weakened immune system get back to normal but also will help to heal any wounds left by the original ich parasites.

Okay, you say you've done all this, and the white spots still persist. At this point we're going to resort to some of the commercially prepared medications made specifically to eradicate ich. Besides following the dosing instructions specifically, make sure you follow these steps in conjunction with administration of medication:

Change 33% of the water prior to each dosing, and 24 hours following the last dose.

Suspend feeding during the dosage period, and gradually raise the aquarium temperature to the mid 80s° F.

This male Black Sailfin Molly is developing a bacterial infection on its lips, on the top of its head close to the base of the dorsal fin and in its eye. The tissue killed by the bacteria will be attacked by fungus in a few days. Photo by Burkhard Kahl.

Remove any carbon filtration during dosing. Carbon will remove the medicinal effect of the treatment.

Lower the temperature back to normal 24 hours following the last dose administered.

Some aquarists recommend the addition of tetracycline following the administration of ich medication to aid in the healing process. I have found the dechlorinators containing soothing and preventive substances to do the same or better...and they're more natural.

One final word on ich. It should not be a foregone conclusion that your mollies will contract ich. You can conclude, however, that if you provide your mollies with inferior water quality or haphazard maintenance they will. The parameters for keeping mollies healthy have already been put forth. These are simple guidelines that will lead you to happy, healthy, ichless mollies. If you do follow everything recommended here, and your fish still come down with ich, or any of the other diseases I'm about to discuss, don't blame yourself too much. Sometimes fish get sick regardless of how well we think we care for them.

This Black Sphenops Molly is developing mouth fungus. Photo by Edward Taylor.

FUNGUS

If you go to view your beautiful sailfin mollies and you notice what looks like a cottonball on the tailfin, or any other part of this fish's body for that matter, you're probably looking at a fungal infection. Mostly you will notice these cottony outgrowths around the tail or mouth region of the fish. Where did they come from? More likely than not, they are the result of poor water quality or wounds that allow a fungus of some type to attack the fish's flesh.

There are supposed to be well over 50,000 species of fungus. When you hear that cute little saying, "There's a fungus among us," it's truer than you thought. For the purposes of this book, we're going to stick with a particular species that seems to affect mollies and many other tropical fish the most: *Saprolegnia.*

The onset of the *Saprolegnia* fungus, a white to yellowish-gray growth, is often brought on by decay. The decay can be a direct or indirect result of a dead and decomposing fish in the aquarium. It can also come about from decaying foodstuffs in and about the aquarium. If this is the case I can tell you right now you're a chronic overfeeder. Knock it off. Your fish don't need nearly that much food.

All right, so you can see how a fungus happens to attack food or a dead fish, but how does it make its way onto the free-swimming fish in your tank? Simple. Poor water quality. Poor water quality adversely affects your fish's immune system, and having a weakened immune system makes it harder for the fish to fight off a fungal attack. A lot of the parasites and malady-causers are forever present in and around your aquarium, but healthy fishes often are able to ward off their attacks. It's the weak fishes that become much more susceptible to infection.

While fungus is treatable, it is not as easily eradicated as ich. There are fungus remedies on the market. Check with a trusted pet store professional for a suitable fungus remedy and make sure that you follow the directions provided on the container the remedy comes in.

If you adhere to the procedures recommended in conjunction with the specific dosing instructions, the fungus should gradually disappear within a week's time. If a week has gone by and the fungus is disappearing but not

Poecilia sphenops, the 24-Carat Gold Molly (female). Fish produced by Ekk-Will. Photo by Edward Taylor.

completely gone, give it a few more days. Some infections are tougher than others. If after 10 days or so your problem persists, you may want to consult an aquarium professional for stronger measures.

FIN ROT

If I sound like a broken record when I say that fin rot, too, is more than likely caused by poor water quality, then take heed. *Most* fish ailments are caused by unacceptable water conditions in the aquarium. I keep over 25 aquariums in my home and rarely are fish medications part of my budget.

This swordtial has lost most of its tail to fin rot. Photo by Ruda Zukal.

If you're crying "*but my water is perfect,*" there is, perhaps another reason. Now this cause does not often affect mollies, as they are swift movers in the aquarium. There is always the chance though that there is a bully in the tank nipping at your mollies' fins.

This activity combined with an increased stress level can certainly bring about fin rot. What exactly is fin rot, anyway?

Actually it is what it sounds like, and it's quite easily detectable. The fins look as if they are rotting away. Instead of having smooth edges, they are tattered and worn looking. Additionally you may encounter red streaks running through the fins, especially the caudal (tail) fin. Sometimes secondary bacterial infections and/or fungus may result from the fin rot. If not treated the fins will eventually completely degenerate, and the fish will perish not only from greatly lessened mobility but a perilous stress level as well. Luckily, fin rot is treatable.

First, make sure the fin rot is not being caused by fin nippers. Many mollies find themselves in community tanks with chronic fin-nippers like tiger barbs (*Capoeta tetrazona*). While these little fish are curious and amusing they are often major league fin nippers, especially when kept singly and not in schools of 5 or 6. If you have a tiger barb or two in with your mollies (not a very good idea to begin with, because tiger barbs don't like the water conditions that mollies thrive in) remove either the mollies or the tiger barbs, or try adding several more tigers to your tank to keep the one or two you have already company. They will generally chase each other when provided with more of their own kind to school with. I use tiger barbs as my prime example because they often tend to be the culprits, but the same can hold true for other fish, be they large or small. So keep an

Poecilia velifera, the Black Veiltail Molly (male) whose elongated gonopodium (modified anal fin used for reproduction) is useless but it is now being attacked by fungus. Photo by Edward Taylor.

eye out. One nighttime felon is often the spotted pim catfish (*Pimelodus pictus*).

If fin nippers aren't the cause, you have to go back and check on your water.

Curing the fish of fin rot is feasible through the use of commercially available remedies. Obtain your dealer's recommended medication and use it strictly according to directions. After the treatment period is over, you'd probably be well advised to treat the aquarium water with one of the products that contain stress-reducing substances designed to help to build up the immune systems of fishes. Use the stress-reduction product on a weekly basis until you see the fins beginning to regenerate. At that point you can resume your normal maintenance routines.

It can sometimes take months for the fins to return to normal, depending on the severity of the damage. Many times an affected fin loses its true shape to some degree, and it is not unusual for the fin to be blemished as well. There is not much you can do about these imperfections, but it should help you to know that they are of no harm to the fish.

DROPSY

Once again the villain is bad water conditions. Rarely do fish in an aquarium that is given the proper care become stricken with dropsy, or pinecone disease. This isn't to say you can't introduce it into your tank by introducing an infected fish, so always take care when purchasing new specimens. It will also be of extreme benefit to have a quarantine tank available.

What exactly is dropsy? More than likely dropsy is a bacterial or viral infection brought about by a breakdown in the fish's immune system. Usually the cause is poor nutrition or stress. If you think you have been feeding your fish improperly, do your best to improve their diet. It is probably too late for the affected fish, but maybe not so for the others.

Dropsy is characterized by several symptoms, the most noticeable being raised scales.

This is where the name pinecone disease comes from. The scales raise up to such proportions that they often give

Poecilia velifera, the Sunset Lyretail Balloon Molly (male) which was produced by the 5-D Tropical Fish Farm. Photo by Edward Taylor.

the fish the look of a ripe pinecone. Other symptoms include ulcerations about the body and redness and/or swelling about the fish's anal region as well as at the base of the fins. Additionally you may encounter long pale-colored strings of waste. A fish affected with dropsy is not a pretty sight to say the least.

Unfortunately for you, and more so the fish, treatment for dropsy is often a hit and miss situation. The best course of action would be to remove the fish from the aquarium into a tank of its own where it can be quarantined. Make sure the water quality of this tank is of optimal condition. Often a fish suffering from dropsy will not eat, so the suspension of feedings will not be overly detrimental for the next 72 hours or so. Treat the fish with a broad-spectrum antibiotic that is available from your pet store professional. As always when using a medication of any kind, follow the manufacturer's directions very carefully.

If your fish begins to show signs of improvement, begin feeding a high quality diet. Give the fish the best if you want it to recover fully. Make certain all symptoms are gone before considering moving it back to the community aquarium. If not, you may want to consider euthanizing the fish.

POP-EYE (EXOPHTHALMIA)

I have to admit that this was one of the first diseases I encountered as a junior hobbyist keeping mollies before I knew about the importance of salt in the aquarium (early 1970's). I was quite "grossed-out" to see my prized chocolate-chip sailfin molly swimming around with one eye protruding from his head like some sort of monster in a horror movie. Yikes! The result of my inability to properly treat, or more importantly prevent, this occurrence literally led to the fish's eye falling off. Ultimately this fish died, but luckily for me no one else came down with the disease. What brought this on to begin with? You guessed it...poor water quality. There are other factors that could lead to this *"unsightly"* disease. Bacterial infections and parasitic infestations are also causal agents of pop-eye. Most cases, however, stem from the fish's being kept in unfavorable conditions. Usually mollies kept in poor water will come down with ich first. If you manage to cure that but persist with bad maintenance practices, an outbreak of pop-eye surely could occur.

If your molly has pop-eye it's pretty simple to tell. Whereas a healthy molly's eye will form a nicely smoothed convex curve just above the skull, a case of pop-eye will shoot the eye or eyes several millimeters above the skull, depending on the severity of the disease. My molly's eye raised about 4 millimeters over its head. Considering the size of the fish, this was a considerable manifestation.

While pop-eye is not a rapidly spreading disease, it would be a good idea to isolate the victim in a

A pair of healthy Salt-and-Pepper Mollies. The male is the lower fish. Photo by Andre Roth.

This *Poecilia sphenops* is an example of a Sunburst Molly with some Comet showing in the tail (unusual for mollies). Fish produced by Moonlight Fishery and photographed by Edward Taylor.

separate aquarium. The next step would be to carefully examine the water quality in the fish's original tank, and immediately take appropriate measures to relieve any abnormalities. If you check your water and find that there are no gross abnormalities with regard to the usual factors, your case of pop-eye may have been caused by a bacterial infection. If this is the case, the pop-eye may be treatable. If not, monitor the affected fish for other outward signs of stress that may eventually require euthanasia. Sometimes the fish will recover, but the abnormal characteristics of the pop-eye's effect may remain. Or the eye falls off, but the fish is fine otherwise.

If you want to try to treat the pop-eye as a bacterial infection, you want to medicate with a wide-spectrum antibiotic. These medicines are usually available at almost any aquarium store.

I know I've done a lot of finger-pointing in this chapter. I've blamed you for all of your fish's

Poecilia velifera, the Green Sailfin Molly (male) produced by Blackwater Fishery and photographed by Edward Taylor.

ailments and woes. But water is so much more than just a familiar liquid. It's hydrogen. It's oxygen. It's dissolved salts. It has mineral content. It has good bacteria, and it has bad bacteria. Your job is to do your best to give your fish as perfect a watery environment as possible. That's not to say that your fish can't get sick even if you do everything right. Some of them are going to get sick no matter what you do and no matter how hard you try. But the more you know about all of these things the better chance you have of avoiding ailments. The longer you keep fish, the more you will find that their woes have a tendency to become your woes. You'll also find the more experience you have, the fewer disease situations you'll encounter. Keeping up water quality becomes second nature to you, to the point that you eventually acquire a "wet thumb."

THE QUARANTINE TANK

Keeping an *"extra"* aquarium in your home just in case a fish gets sick may seem like a superfluous gesture, but it's really quite practical. Actually a simply set up aquarium that you can keep in almost any out-of-the-way place can come in quite handy even if you're not experiencing disease or illness. You can use it, for example, as a place in which to segregate newly acquired fish to observe them for potential diseases before you introduce them to your main tank. Many of us keeping nicely arranged communities of fish are often left shattered when a diseased fish infects our entire aquarium. Fish sometimes harbor diseases and/ or infections that are not always visible to the naked eye. If you have the wherewithal to keep the fish separated from the community after the initial purchase is made, any latent maladies will more than likely pop up during the recommended two-week quarantining period.

Should a fish within your community fall victim to one of the aforementioned diseases, or any other for that matter, you may find medicating the specimen necessary. If you read the dosage amounts on the medication packages you will see that the dosages are based on the gallonage of water. If you have one sick fish in a 55-gallon aquarium, this can become an expensive proposition. Additionally you are needlessly (and potentially harmfully) medicating otherwise healthy fish. The more practical approach would be to place the affected fish in the quarantine, or hospital, tank. More than likely this will be a smaller tank, depending on the average size of the fish you keep. This way you are treating only the affected fish, plus it's much easier to keep a watchful eye on the distressed patient. Remember as well that the sick fish is a weakened fish. Kept in a tank full of healthy residents, the fish may be preyed upon. A hospital tank lets you help out.

Another good use for this quarantine tank is to temporarily house tank bullies. Many fish become quite territorial in their little glass homes, some so much so that they batter any tankmate who comes even close to their staked-out domain. One way to combat this situation is to remove the fish from its territory and let others take over. When replaced one week later, this fish is no longer dominant and will have—at least for a while—lost the ability to bully its tankmates.

Have I talked you into it yet? Well, let me point out that the hospital tank can and should be simple and cheap. Aha...I'm getting somewhere now! Yes, your hospital/quarantine tank need not be an elaborate set-up. As a

Balloon Silver Mollies. Photo by MP&C Piednoir Aqua Press.

matter of fact, it should be as spartan as possible, with the most attention being paid to the water. Unless you have very large fish, a 10-gallon tank with no gravel should suffice. Place into the tank a foam filter that you allowed to age in your regular community tank for about 30 days. This filter will then serve to break down any of the fish's waste while it is in this tank.

If your quarantine tank is in a high-traffic area of your home you should also provide a little refuge in the tank. This can be accomplished through the use of plastic plants, a piece of driftwood, or a clay flowerpot. New or sick fish can also be somewhat skittish, so it would be a good idea to cover the tank as well. Don't forget to heat the water to the proper temperature. Do your best to have this tank ready for action at a moment's notice. Time can be of the essence, so a delay while your water attains the proper temperature or pH level can be costly.

Keep a notebook by this tank too. You'd be amazed at how quickly you can forget when you medicated, how you medicated, and when to medicate next. Jotting these items down will help you in correctly dosing your fish throughout the treatment period. It doesn't hurt to make notes of the fish's progress. If you are going to quarantine new purchases, write down the date of your new acquisition. It's nice to know when it's safe to put the new fish into the home tank. We all have so much on our minds these days. Give yourself a memory break by putting these little tidbits of information into writing.

Poecilia sphenops, the 24-Carat Lyretail Gold Molly (female). Produced by Ed Parker Tropicals. Photo by Edward Taylor.

Poecilia velifera, the Green Lyretail Sailfin Molly (male) produced by Buzbee's Tropical Fish Farm and photographed by Edward Taylor.

EUTHANASIA

No matter how much love, care and attention we give our fish, there comes a time when we have to make a life or death decision regarding the status of a diseased or failing fish. The decision is hard, but there really is no way to avoid making it.

When a fish is past any reasonable point of recovery, its distress becomes quite obvious.

It becomes listless and will usually hover in a corner of the tank. If it is in a tank with other fish, they will usually begin to pick on it, instinctively realizing its vulnerability. Its fins can become torn and ragged, and it will stop feeding. All of these scenarios are going to lead to the fish's demise no matter what you do for it. So what do you do?

Almost every fishkeeper, at one time or another, has to face the mercy killing of one of their fish. Fortunately you can perform this task and still remain a law-abiding citizen.

Flushing a sick fish down the toilet certainly is not a very merciful means of destroying it. There are several more humane ways to effectively euthanize the fish: they include immersing it in boiling water, immersing it in freezing water, immersing it in water treated with carbon dioxide and even swiftly smashing it on the head. These all work, but I don't like any of them, especially if kids are around.

I have found the most effective and gentle means of performing this function to be the *freeze-to-sleep* method. Wet several paper

Poecilia velifera, the Red Sunset Sailfin Molly (female). Fish produced by Moonlight Fishery and photographed by Edward Taylor.

towels and fold them so they can be wrapped around the fish's body. Net the fish and place it in this wet blanket. Cover the fish completely and place it in a plastic bag, then place this makeshift coffin in your freezer. The freezing will cause the fish's metabolism to gradually slow down, placing it in a deep comatose condition until it freezes to death. This is virtually painless to the fish, and to the performer of this task as well. If young children are part of this ritual, the frozen bag can be buried if appropriate. This is often the very first, and perhaps the very best, way to give children their first introduction to death and dying with minimal trauma.

Poecilia velifera, the Golden Albino Sailfin Molly (male). Produced by Moonlight Fishery and photographed by Edward Taylor.

BREEDING MOLLIES

Breeding mollies can be a very simple exercise, or it can be quite a complex one. The decision will be yours. Whichever road you choose to take, you are certain to reap rewards of enjoyment and fulfillment. If you have children the breeding of mollies can very well supplant the "birds and bees" speech.

The simplest way to breed mollies is to put a male together with a female in the right water conditions, and voila! In 30 days or so your female should be ready to deliver. When you're making your molly selection, however, how does one differentiate a boy from a girl molly? Don't they all look alike? Actually, no. The term "sexually dimorphic" refers to the qualities that visibly differentiate one sex from the other. Mollies are sexually dimorphic. Many other fishes are not. Adult male mollies have a rod-like copulatory organ called a gonopodium situated on the lower belly area; the gonopodium is a modification of the anal fin. The female, as well as young males that have not yet developed sexually, has a regular anal fin.

In adult mollies the females are usually somewhat larger than the males, and females that are well advanced in carrying young are easily distinguished by their overly rotund bellies. Some females also exhibit a dark spot, the so-called gravid spot, on their lower abdomen, just ahead of the anal fin. Adult males, especially adult male *P. velifera* and *P. latipinna*, also show much more orange and yellow-orange coloring on the chest area than adult females do.

Now that you know how to insure purchasing at least one male and one female molly, you're ready to start your molly family. What is the best way to do this? The simplest means would be to put a pair together and watch what happens. Keep in mind that if your mollies are in a tank with other fishes, the resultant live-born young will be treated as tasty morsels and will soon be gone. Not only will the other fishes feast on the babies, but so too will the parents.

The best way to insure a healthy batch of fry is to separate the female in a tank of her own when she shows signs of pregnancy. Remember, a slightly ballooned abdomen or that distinctive black spot will be indicative of this condition. A 2 $^1/_2$ gallon tank will serve this purpose just fine. As horrifying as it may sound, mollies often will eat their fry after birth, although mollies in geneal are less cannibalistic than many other livebearing species. To ensure you are able to bring some of the babies up, you obviously want to separate the mother from the babies as soon as possible after delivery.

A pair of albino *Poecilia velifera.* The female, to the right, has a swollen belly indicating imminent delivery of her living young. Photo by Burkhard Kahl.

There are several ways to do this. One way is to use one of the breeding traps on the market. Unfortunately, mollies are much less able than other livebearers to stand confinement in a breeding trap. Probably the best alternative is to use one of the mats of artificial " grass" that give the newly born fry refuge from the mother molly. This is not a perfect method of securing the fry. They can and will swim out of the grass, but it does give you some extra time to get the mother out of the tank. If you take her out of the tank, don't be in too much of a rush to put her back into the main tank. She should be allowed to rest up for a week or so before being put back into the company of the males, which would surely be after her constantly in attempts to breed.

A molly baby BEFORE it was born. Their yolk sacs are usually absorbed before the babies are born. Photo by Hans Joachim Richter.

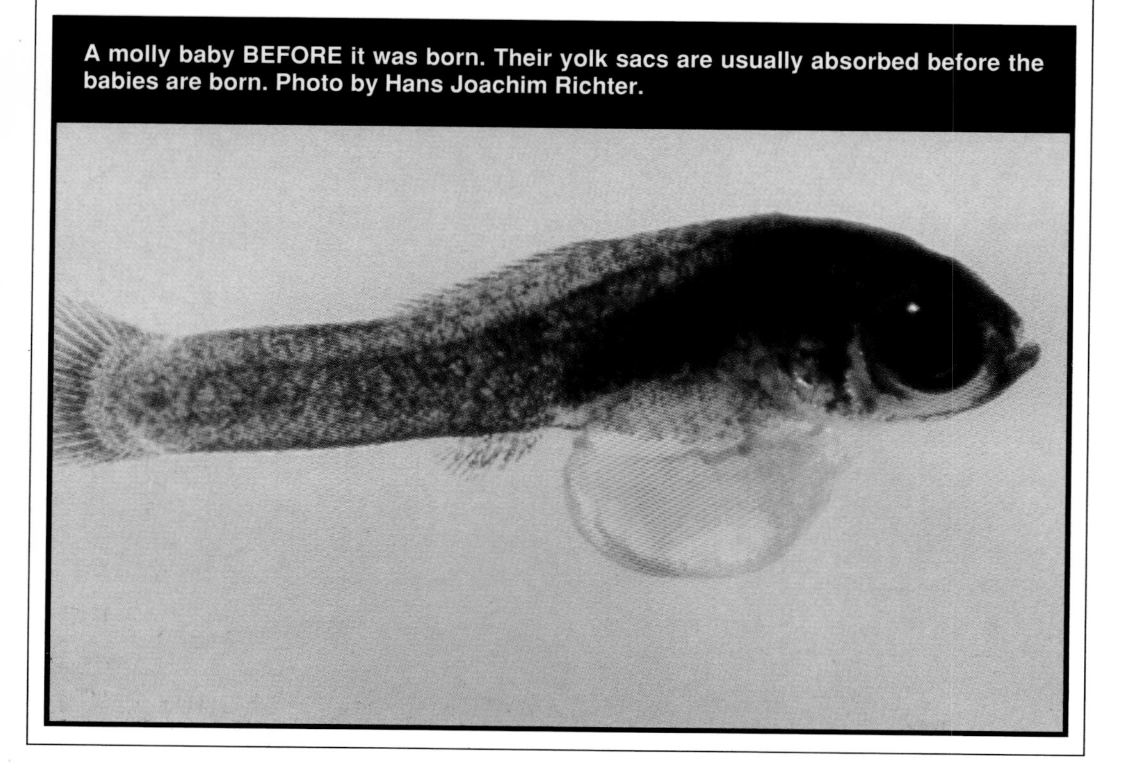

Poecilia latipinna, the Sunburst Molly. The two uppermost fish are females while the lower fish is a male. Females are easily recognized by their larger bellies and more hefty physique. Photo by Dr. Herbert R. Axelrod.

Black Balloon Mollies with lyretails required 3 years of inbreeding and selective breeding to fix the balloon characteristic, then another 2 years to put the lyretail on the fish.

FIXING A STRAIN

Many experienced livebearer enthusiasts would be aghast at the suggestion of merely putting a pair of fish together to do their thing. How gauche! These are people who have spent considerable time and energy developing and fixing strains of livebearers so that they remain healthy and viable specimens. When these strains reach the general public, they are usually met with much enthusiasm and popularity.

The color variations seen in mollies were developed from the generally seen wild color forms of mollies: black and greenish-brown. It was those aquarists, professional and amateur alike, who developed the strains and color variations that are so prominent in mollies today. It might be these folks who would never suggest throwing a pair together. To them this would be tantamount to pedigreed dog owners promoting the breeding of mongrels. But for you there's still a lot to learn by keeping things simple. Maybe once you've gotten a taste for these beautiful livebearers you may even develop a desire to expand your interest...maybe even come up with your own color variety. Personally, I'm still waiting for the turquoise molly to pop up in my tanks.

The scope of this book will not allow me to go into any depth with regard to genetics. One thing you should know, however, before starting your own molly breeding farm, is that your beginning stock is very important. You must start with virgin females to have any success in *"fixing"* a color or strain. Fixing is the term used to describe the ability for the species to consistently and reliably produce offspring of the same type and quality. The need for starting with virgin females results from the fact that female mollies can store sperm packets that can fertilize her eggs long after the initial mating. If your goal is to fix a color strain of "blue" and you mate your female with a male you think can throw "blue" it will be of little consequence if the female is holding sperm of a male that is "purple." Of course, neither of these colors has ever been produced, but who knows? Maybe you'll be the one to do it.

The best way to guarantee the virginity of your female breeding stock is to produce your own. Even if you purchase young females at a store, those showing no signs of gravidity, you still can not be assured that they have not been impregnated.

When purchasing your initial brooding stock (the fish from which you eventually want to start your own breeding program), choose specimens that look sturdy and have color that is

Poecilia velifera, the Sunset Lyretail Balloon Molly (female). The fish was produced by 5-D Fish Farm and photographed by Edward Taylor.

A pair of Harlequin Mollies. The male is the uppermost fish. Derived from *Poecilia sphenops*, this strain was produced by Moonlight Fishery and photographed by Edward Taylor.

devoid of any blemishes. Try to obtain males and females from different sources. This will help guarantee that you are not going to breed brother and sister. You can breed brother and sister later on, but from the outset this would not be the genetically correct thing to do.

Feed your newly acquired mollies well. The best thing to put them in prime breeding condition would be live foods combined with good prepared foods formlated for use with mollies and other vegetarian fishes. Keep them on this for at least a week.

Now if you're set on seriously breeding mollies, you really need to give them a tank of their own. Breeding fish in a community tank becomes an effort in futility. A 10-gallon tank will do nicely for one pair. Once the female is gravid, remove the male. This will lessen the chance of cannibalization once the babies are born, especially if you're not around during the event. You can assume gravidity by the presence of a newly bulged abdomen on the female. Once the babies are born, remove the mother. Keep track of who she is and what type of spawn was thrown in combination with a specific male. This information is vital to any true breeding program.

Black Mollies look great in a shallow indoor pool and several airports (especially Singapore) feature these fish because of their contrast to the bottom of the pool and their habit of staying close to the surface of the water.

FEEDING THE BABIES

Upon birth, your newly born mollies can easily slurp up finely ground dry food. What you have to watch out for is overfeeding. This habit can lead quickly to fouling the water and should be avoided by all means. Look at it this way. There are going to be more babies than you know what to do with. (Or at least that's the case with a fully adult large female; younger females that are giving birth for only the first or second time generally have many fewer young.) Let nature do its thing. Feed sparsely, letting the strong survive. This leads us to the subject of *culling.*

CULLING

Defined bluntly, culling is the operation of separating the worthless from the worthy. Now you may look upon your first brood, and even subsequent broods, as being the light of your life. This is O.K., if that's what you want, a never-ending houseful of mollies. But if your intention is to formulate a solid breeding program, capable of producing as many high quality fish as possible, you want to grow to maturity only your finest stock. This selection process requires doing away with the less than suitable fish. If you have larger fish-eating fishes, the less than average babies can be fed to them. Otherwise you may want to utilize one of the

Mollies bear their young internally. The young, when delivered, are self supporting and free swimming. Black Mollies, like the one shown here, deliver little Black Molly babies which are identical to their parents providing their parents are both Black Mollies. Molly parents often eat their own babies unless the babies have a place to hide in thick vegetation. Special traps are also available at pet shops to save the young from their parents. Photo by Dr. Herbert R. Axelrod.

methods of euthanasia described earlier.

What traits do you want to look for when deciding which fry to keep and raise and which ones to cull? This will take some experience on your part. In the beginning, look for the obvious. Study pictures and descriptions of the adult fish, checking into what an optimal specimen looks like. As the fry grow you will see obvious strengths and weaknesses. Cull out the bent fins, the curved spines, the runts not keeping pace with the rest of their brood. Those fish will only pass on their undesirable traits. Instead, keep the strong, vibrantly colored fish. Look for those keeping their fins erect and eating heartily. As they grow and you can begin to tell the difference between the sexes, separate out the females. This is how you ensure yourself some virgin female stock.

RAISING THE FRY

Fortunately, newborn mollies are large enough that they can be given foods easily obtainable.

A pair of Lyretail Black Mollies. The lyretail makes them distinctive. The over-developed anal fin often impedes fertilization.

Flake food crushed between the thumb and forefinger or pushed through a sieve is certainly suitable. If you want, you can purchase the food already crushed. This is often labeled as livebearer fry food.

A supplemental food that is simple enough to prepare would be the yolk of a hard-boiled egg. Push a small piece of the yolk through a fine piece of cloth, such as a good linen handkerchief. Rub the pulverized yolk off the hanky and into the water. The babies will usually swim through the yolky cloud making pigs of themselves. Remember, however, that the egg yolk is just a supplemental feeding; don't use it as your staple diet. The commercially prepared fish foods are better for that.

It's a good idea to give your little fish as many as five to six feedings a day. I know that that's not always easy to do, but certainly it's easy enough to give a minimum of two separate feedings a day, one in the morning and one in the evening. To make sure all fish are getting a significant portion of food per feeding, you do want to feed more voluminously. This act will absolutely require frequent water changes, however.

In order to facilitate optimal growth and lessen the chance of disease, water changes are of utmost importance. You should

Poecilia sphenops, the Liberty Molly has been around as an aquarium fish for at least 78 years. This is a female; the males are slightly more colorful. Fish produced by Quality Critters and photographed by Edward Taylor.

A pair of albino Lyretail Mollies. The male is the lower fish. They derived from *Poecilia velifera.* Produced by Ekk-Will and photographed by Edward Taylor.

really try to change half of the water volume every other day. Keeping the babies in a 2 1/2- or 5-gallon tank makes this chore easier. At this point you want to try to keep water that has been allowed to sit for at least 48 hours after having come out of the tap. And of course you're concerned here not only with having dechlorinated water but also with having water of the correct temperature, say a degree or two warmer than the water you're exchanging it for.

Siphon the water out of the tank using a piece of 3/16" flexible tubing. As the water is being drawn out glide the tube across the bottom of the tank, picking up as much accumulated debris and mulm as possible. Don't worry too much about sucking up babies. Normally as you're cruising the siphon tube across the tank, the babies will scurry to get out of the way. If one does get sucked up by accident, just gently net him out of the vessel he was sucked into. Some folks will recommend rubber-banding a piece of nylon stocking over the end of the tube to prevent this occurrence. Unfortunately, that also prevents any dirt from being sucked out. Just be careful.

THE MOLLIES

As I stated in the beginning of this book, mollies belong to the family Poeciliidae. Within this family are more than 20 described species of the genus *Poecilia*, which includes species not considered to be mollies. And of the mollies, only three are commonly present in the hobby. They were described earlier as: *Poecilia sphenops* (common molly or sphenops molly), *Poecilia latipinna* (sailfin molly), and *Poecilia velifera* (Yucatan sailfin molly).

POECILIA SPHENOPS

Quite possibly, as a beginning hobbyist your first run-in with a livebearer would be a molly of this variety. The quintessential black molly is easily endeared to us for many reasons. In its ubiquitous black form, this molly is an inexpensive, vibrant, active livebearer. Many new and old hobbyists are enthralled by the molly's livebearing status and are compelled to begin with this one for those reasons outlined.

The sphenops molly can be found swimming in natural habitats ranging from the estuarine waters of Mexico through areas of Central America and into the waters of northernmost South America. In this species the female tends to be somewhat larger than the male at adulthood. Females are seen as large as 3 inches (8 cm) while males are somewhat smaller at 2

Wild-caught *Poecilia sphenops*. The fish came from the Rio Palizada, Campeche, Mexico. Photo by Lothar Wischnath.

Poecilia velifera, the Original Gold-dust Molly. This is a pair with the male on the bottom. Produced by Buzbee's Tropical Fish Farm and photographed by Edward Taylor.

to 2 1/2 inches (6 cm). The sphenops molly can do quite well in a community tank set-up provided you don't forget to add that 1 teaspoon of salt per gallon of water.

The sphenops molly has been commercially bred to include a number of very striking colors and color combinations. These would include the white or silver molly. A cross between a black version and a white version could result in what is commonly named the salt & pepper molly, which is actually a spangling of the black and white coloration.

There is the gold dust molly. This would be similar in patterning to the salt & pepper molly except the colors would be a speckling of black and gold (yellow). As there are no true-colored gold sphenops, this color variety was more than likely an outcrossing of a sphenops and a sailfin molly species. The gold dust then became a fixed strain more reminiscent of the sphenops in size and fin shape.

In addition to the color variations, you can often see the sphenops molly with varying fin shapes. The fish's natural finnage would be that of a rounded tail fin and a short dorsal fin. The male's dorsal fin is somewhat larger than the female's. The male is also distinguishable from the female by the adapted anal fin which serves as the male's copulatory organ, the gonopodium.

One of these man-made versions would be the lyre-tail. As you can see by the photos of this variety the tail has points from the upper and lower rays that jut out significantly, giving it a lyre-like appearance. In some cases man has played around a little too much with the finnage. Some of this "toying" has resulted in males with oversized gonopodiums which are rendered useless for breeding purposes. In these cases it is almost impossible to "fix" a strain of this sort by virtue of the fish's inability to copulate.

All of these color and/or tail fin varieties make excellent aquarium inhabitants. They are hearty eaters and will accept most aquarium fare.

THE BALLOON MOLLY

While the balloon molly is purely man-made (so to speak) and has no separate speciation, it is still a familiar morph in the aquarium hobby. If you look at the photographs of this molly, you can see how its body size and coloration are quite similar to that of *P. sphenops*. More than likely, it was in fact a cross between the sphenops and another species of molly. This cross produced a small molly with an extremely distended abdominal cavity.

The care required for these fish should be the same as that of *P. sphenops*. Care should be exercised, however, when keeping them in a community tank with swift aggressively feeding fish. Their abdominal distension sometimes makes approaching food in a competitive manner an awkward proposition. Some balloons have no problem at all. Just keep an eye out so they get their fair share.

The original strain of Green Balloon Mollies did not have the grotesque appearance that some of them now have.

Two male Albino Sailfin Mollies. Photo by Mark Smith.

POECILIA LATIPINNA

Broad fin. That's what the Latin species designation of this fish stands for. The name is quite indicative of the male's large dorsal fin. This is a much larger fish than *P. sphenops*, not just in finnage, but overall body size as well. A male *P. latipinna* can attain an adult size of 3 inches (8cm) while the female of the species has been known to top the charts at 4 inches (10 cm). Aquarium specimens generally do not maximize their size potential as in the wild, yet their size still remains impressive compared to other molly species.

These sailfins hail from the southeastern coasts of the United States, down and through the Yucatan peninsula of southeast Mexico. Here they enjoy the many variations of water from quite saline to completely fresh.

In their wild state, *P. latipinna* is of an olive coloration, darker on top, lighter down below. The dorsal fin and upper body flanks are adorned with shimmering dots running horizontally from the base of the skull through the tail fin. Some males have an orange chest, perhaps leading to the solid gold color form (orange like a goldfish) often available for sale. Sailfins of this species have been bred to put forth not only the greenish natural color and the gold, but several other body colors

Weird genetics mark these *Poecilia latipinna*. They are colored in black and gold and brown. Yet they have red eyes! The genetics of this occurrence has never been explained. Photo by Michael Gilroy of fish from Scotland.

as well. Other color forms available are solid black, salt & pepper, and white (sometimes called silver).

Poecilia latipinna is similar to the other sailfin molly, *Poecilia velifera*, and can be hard to tell apart. Both make good community tank residents, though they should definitely be kept in pairs in order to fully appreciate their splendor as they sail through the tank in tandem.

POECILIA VELIFERA

This fish is found solely in the Yucatan Peninsula. If you look at the shape of the dorsal fin of a male *P. latipinna* you will see that it is shaped triangularly. In the relaxed state it resembles a scalene triangle. When the fish is excited and the fin is fully erect it looks like an inverted equilateral triangle.

A *P. velifera* male's dorsal fin is more rectangular in shape and

The top fish is a male Sunburst Molly derived from *Poecilia sphenops*. The bottom fish is a male Red Sunset Sailfin Molly derived from *Poecilia velifera*. The fish were produced by Moonlight Fishery and photographed by Edward Taylor.

Poecilia velifera, the Silver Molly (female). Fish produced by Buzbee's Tropical Fish Farm and photographed by Edward Taylor.

Poecilia velifera, the Black Lyretail Molly (male). Fish produced by Buzbee's Tropical Fish Farm and photographed by Edward Taylor.

can rise almost 2 inches (5cm) above the spine. The species designation "velifera" translates from Latin to mean "carrying a sail." And that it certainly does. When you combine this magnificent canvas with its large size, you certainly have one impressive fish.

P. velifera is the largest of the molly species. Literature states the males attain lengths upwards of 6 inches (15cm) while the females hit a lofty size of 8 inches (20cm). I have never seen any of these fish offered for sale or even displayed anywhere near these sizes. Rather you can count on obtaining specimens at an average of 4 inches (10cm). At this size they still are sexually mature and will produce quite prolifically.

Molly breeders, both professional and hobbyist, have also developed very pretty color strains in this fish, all of which are readily available for sale. These colors would include the solids: white (silver), black, often with a matte finish, gold (orange), brown, as well as a green (silvery-olive). Additionally, some very pretty mottlings have been derived by breeding the solid colors to one

Poecilia sphenops, the Ebony and Ivory Molly (female). The fish were produced by Sanchez Brothers Tropical Fish and photographed by Edward Taylor.

Poecilia sphenops, the Salt and Pepper Molly (female). Produced by Moonlight Fishery and photographed by Edward Taylor.

another. These would include: black & white (sometimes labeled as salt & pepper or Dalmatian mollies), and brown & gold (chocolate chip).

All of these color variations are quite beautiful. Don't cheat yourself of their beauty by housing them with minimal lighting. A high quality fluorescent bulb will show off a luster in the scales and fins that is unmatched. It is best to give these fish a tank of their own in order not to overcrowd them. They can sometimes be kept as community fish, though they have known to be nippy towards smaller fish.

For the purposes of this molly primer I chose to highlight mollies available to you, rather than frustrate you with teasers. This is not to say that some rarer species are not available; you just have to do a little leg work to find them...sometimes a lot of leg work.

Poecilia butleri is one of the 20 other fishes in the genus *Poecilia*. Photo by Lothar Wischnath.

The Atlas of Livebearers of the World, by Lothar Wischnath, features all species and subspecies of the genus *Poecilia*. This book, published by T.F.H. Publications, also features many other livebearers that you will certainly find interesting.

There is also a specialty organization known as the American Livebearer Association. This is a group of people who specialize in the keeping and raising of livebearers. Other popular livebearers would include the guppy, the swordtail, the platy, and other not so well known fish. Through membership, one can often garner some of the rarer varieties from other members. Their address can change from year to year, so it doesn't pay to publish it here. Look to *Tropical Fish Hobbyist* magazine for the most recent address.

If you learned one thing at all from this text I expect that it is that the molly is far from a little beginner fish. It has specific needs, both nutritionally and with regard to its habitat. It is a brackish-water fish. If you want it to survive, thrive, and multiply you should add that salt to the aquarium.

If you do develop that turquoise molly, write to me in care of T.F.H. I want a pair!

INDEX

Page numbers in **boldface** refer to illustrations.